WINEMAKING SIMPLIFIED

BY

E. H. CORNISH

WINEMAKING SIMPLIFIED

by

E. H. Cornish

1st Impression 1984

Published by: Amateur Winemaker Publications Ltd.,
South Street, Andover, Hants.

Printed by: Standard Press (Andover) Ltd.,
South Street, Andover, Hants.

ISBN 0 900841 76 1

Dedication: To Christine, who made it all happen.

Contents

Page No.

PHILOSOPHY

Why should you make wine?
I can suggest at least four good reasons . . . .
Because:

You like the taste
You like the processing activity
You want to impress friends
You like the price!

An awful lot of nonsense is put about concerning wine – "pretentious", "full-bodied", "floral" are words often used in descriptions of these ambrosial fluids. People also rave about the correct temperature for drinking it, forgetting that one's response to food and drink varies with state of health, temperament, environment and degree of hunger and thirst at various times. So forget all the nonsense and mystique surrounding any wine which you drink with your meat (who would describe a *steak* as "pretentious", or demand that it be served at 43° Celsius?), and enjoy it just as a drink. You will find that red wines can taste very well at room temperature, and white wines are often good as a cool drink, but do not overdo temperature control. Too long an immersion in the ice bucket can make many a white wine almost tasteless.

Think big: although the drunkenness factor of a one gallon brew is more than for five gallons (because different chemicals, called "esters", occurr in greater amount in small brews), making one gallon at a time means that you will be tempted to drink it too soon. The results may seem good at first, but wine really *does* get better if kept for one, two or even four years. So make a lot, and some will survive in your cellar for a reasonable time before being opened. Even tasting at the rate of one bottle each month means that the last bottle of a ten gallon batch will be five years old.

Don't expect to make wine from any old fruit without using some form of grape as well. *Some* grape content is essential to provide flavour and body. Grape can be in several forms:

Concentrated juice
Raisins
Sultanas
Real grapes (usually uneconomic to use unless you actually grow them).

Don't enter your product in competitions (such as in a Wine Makers club) unless you are very good, as your wine after being tasted may be relegated towards the bottom of the table; this could make you feel bad. Keep the wine for those who will appreciate it – your family.

Drink and enjoy! Live for the moment! It is said, surely truthfully, that a glass of wine a day is good for the digestion, and prolongs life. I'm hoping it will prolong mine . . . .

First tips for the tyro

Wine kits are best to start with, as they are simple to use and only need sugar and yeast to be added (sometimes no sugar if you pay a lot for the kit). Don't despise kits. They make very good wine. Learn the basic manipulations of wine making with kits: wine making involves quite a lot of work but this is least with kits. Once you gain confidence, go for the complexities of using fruit.

Prices of kits vary: those where *you* supply the sugar are cheapest and best to start with. If you are not even able to accomplish simple operations such as weighing out and dissolving the requisite sugar into a volume of liquid, then wine making is not for you – take up lacrosse!

Some kits claim to produce wine which is ready to drink in three months, or some even in three weeks. Don't be tempted – the results may be passable, but you won't be getting the real pay-off which can be achieved when wine making at home. Even kit wine gets better after one year, two years, three years – as it matures, it gets better and better, at least in taste, although some reds have a tendency to turn brown after about four years.

To avoid having to drink your wine too soon, make plenty. Kits and most recipes suggest quantities sufficient to make one gallon. I suggest making five gallons or, better, ten at a time. This would seem to be a big financial investment: it is, so do your work right first time and encourage yourself by finding out how much you would pay for ten gallons from a shop.

Failures are always expensive in wine-making, both in materials and man-hours. To avoid failures:

Read and learn from this book.

Start with kits and abide by their instructions.

Don't go on to using fruit for wine making until you are practised in the basic manipulations.

Follow the cardinal rule "keep everything and every process *CLEAN*".

You will find the important parts in later Chapters.

Equipment you need

"Equipment" means hardware you will use over and over again. "Materials" are consumables such as sugar, other edibles, corks, caps and labels.

Remember that you also need space, more than you might think. Hard-surfaced wipe-down working tops are good; so is a fair-sized sink. You will always spill liquids on the floor. Most of these are sticky, so avoid mats and carpets underfoot.

For fermentation vessels on a small scale, use one gallon glass demijohns. The most useful are those having a neck with ring-type handles, which are intended to help with picking-up. They are also useful for holding on to when swilling round for cleaning, and act as a convenient holder for your production record (see later).

Get the clear glass ones always, as the yeast will work in light as well as in the dark, as long as an airlock is used. Amber bottles look special, but you cannot see when the yeast has settled at the end of the process. Also you cannot see where the end of the siphon tube is, and you cannot easily check for cleanliness. A problem with demijohns is that they are hard to clean around the shoulder – use a bottle brush (essential) bent to shape, or else buy a specially-shaped brush for the job.

Another disadvantage of the demijohn is the narrow neck. It is wide enough if you are making wine from a kit, as all the "must" is a liquid. Should you be using chopped-up fruit, getting it into the neck can be a problem equalled only by that of getting it out later.

For five gallon brews, use a plastic container like those used for camping water supplies. Be sure to buy those suitable for food use, not once-used containers which contained agricultural sprays or the like. Do not use metal containers at all as they can corrode and taint the wine.

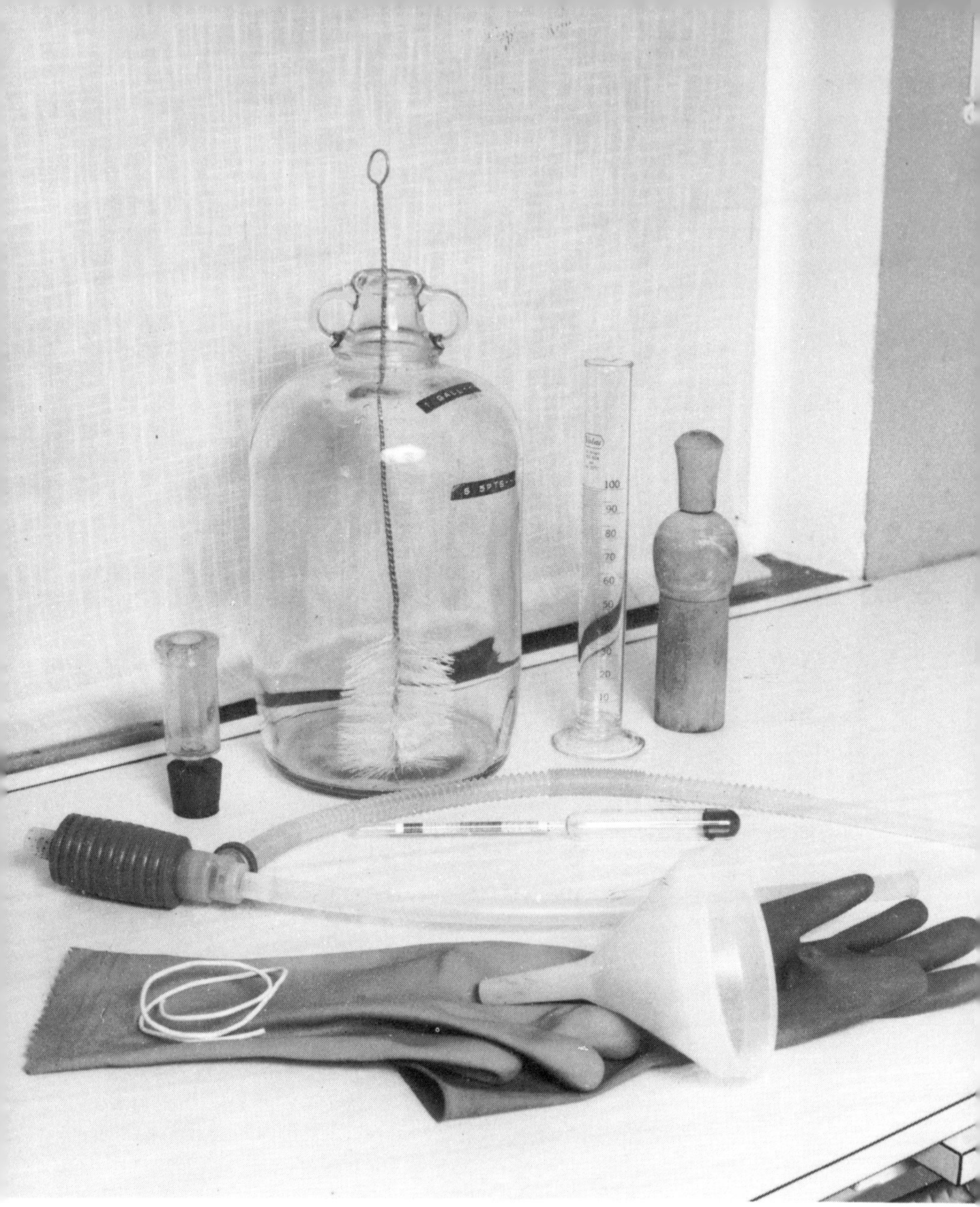

Small kit: glass demijohn, cleaning brush, fermentation lock in bung, hydrometer jar, corker, hydrometer, siphon, rubber gloves and funnel.

In any event, choose a five gallon container with fairly wide mouth, say two inches minimum diameter. Then when you make apple wine (you will some time – it is not at all like cider), the crushed apples will go into the neck for soaking and flavour extraction, and can easily be shaken out later.

These five gallon containers are hard to clean: I use household bleach at the rate of two cups to five gallons of water, and soak for a day or two. Much of the crud comes off with a brush, but if possible use the brush before the bleach. At the end of all this there may still be visible stains through the container, especially on the underside of the top; ignore them.

Airlocks are made of plastic or of glass; it doesn't matter which you use as they are all very difficult to clean. Both can be broken. A plastic airlock will show straight lines of crazing after some use, but these do not matter. Do not fill airlocks with Campden or bisulphite solution during use, as you are advised to do in many books. Such practice is the received wisdom, but I never find it necessary. Use clean water, and top it up or change it now and again during a fermentation. Campden solution, should you overfill the lock, as is likely at first, might suck back into the "must" and could kill or at least weaken the yeast.

Fit airlocks to the necks of fermentation vessels with rubber bungs, not corks. Bungs fit better, are more airtight and are *much* easier to keep clean than a cork.

A two or three gallon bucket is useful for extracting flavour from fruit. Many recipes call for covering fruit with boiling water, cooling, adding ingredients and fermenting on the pulp for up to two weeks. A bucket can well be used at first, but to extract flavour well, pieces of fruit should always be small enough to pass through the two inch neck of the five gallon fermentation vessel – so in a day or so (when the liquid has cooled) transfer to *that*.

Do not be tempted to allow your wine fermentation to take place in a beer fermentation vessel, unless the lid fits well enough to exclude *all* oxygen from the air, there is always the risk that you might finish up by making high class vinegar . . . . (although I do this at times, and have always got away with it) However, the rule still holds good.

Bottles can be purchased from do-it-yourself wine maker's displays in chemists or specialist shops, but are prohibitively expensive. When the wine-making bug bites, look at your own reserves of empty wine

A larger fermenter: it must have an airtight lid that can be fitted with an air lock.

bottles (you must sometimes have bought a bottle, or how else did you discover your liking for it?) and also put the message out amongst your friends. If friends fail you, hang around the back doors of pubs, wine shops, wine bars and banquetting halls. If you go to a banquet or other large scale meal, have a word with a wine waiter. A modest honorarium will produce a case of empty bottles at the end of the evening. The local Church may have a store of empty sacramental wine bottles – get to know a Churchwarden or even the Vicar! If you are able to organise matters so that freshly-emptied bottles will come your way, ask the lucky drinker to rinse out the liquid dregs. Dried wine residue in a bottle is very difficult to get off: it it is left there it could be detrimental to the new wine.

Bottles to use. **Bottles to avoid.**

Do not use lemonade, sherry, champagne or screw-capped bottles. Corks will not fit these odd-shaped necks very well, and screw caps themselves are not much good at excluding air over long periods. Furthermore your product will look amateurish in such bottles. Even when well presented, you may have to explain your wine to friends!

White bottles are the least common, green being most usual and pale green and mid-brown less so. The shape or colour do not matter much for home-made wine (although a purist might use a particular bottle for a simulated named wine). It does not matter either if the bottles have punts (upward-pointing dimples in the bottom) or not, as any sediment formed on storage (and there usually will be *some*) will be too light to settle firmly into the space available. However, if you use pure grapes for the wine, the tartar deposit from *them* is quite heavy and crystalline, so will stay at the bottom anyway when you come to pouring out. It is useful to bottle the whole of a batch of wine in the same shapes or at least the same colours of bottle, as an aid to identification in the cellar. There you can group all the bottles of a batch together, so as to avoid looking at every label to find the type you want.

How you store bottles depends of course on available space. A rack can be made out of two sheets of 8 foot by 4 foot chipboard held apart by four inch thick timber. When suitably bored by using a power drill and cup saws (a small one for the bottle neck and a larger one for the bottle base), such a rack, when securely fixed a few inches from a wall, can hold upwards of 200 bottles on their sides. Cardboard cartons (from wine shops) which take 12 or 15 bottles can be laid on their sides if full, but are not good otherwise unless you fill the remaining spaces with empty bottles. They can be stacked upright at least to four cartons high, but the corks might dry out unless good grade, well-fitting ones are used.

Filters come in many forms and prices. Some people always filter their wine; others, like me, only if they have to. If a wine is cloudy with a pectin or starch haze, *no* filter will clear it, and you must have recourse to blending or some other palliative as explained later.

Pectin might be present in the "must" from many kinds of fruit, so you add pectolytic enzyme to destroy it, otherwise an intractable haze is formed. Test for pectin (perhaps to check completion of the enzyme treatment) by putting a dessert-spoon of the "must" in a clear glass, adding four similar measures of methylated spirit or medical alcohol,

Bottle storage rack made from two parallel sheets of chipboard.

and stirring. The liquid will become more cloudy than before, and will drop down a loose, fluffy deposit if you have no problem. If pectin is present in significant amount, then blobs or strings of jelly will soon form and cling to the glass. Double check with a finger that it really is sticky. Do *not* return this test sample to your ''must''.

A starch haze may derive from overboiled starting materials, such as potatoes or wheat, and may be confused with a pectin or protein haze. To test for starch, put a little of the ''must'' into a clear glass and add two drops of tincture of iodine. In a few minutes, a white or rosé wine will show a dull, dark blue colour if starch is present. In the case of a red wine, add twice as much iodine and allow to stand for an hour. Carefully pour off as much wine as possible and add clear water to the residue in the glass. If much starch is present, you will detect the blue colour; if not, you still won't know!

If the wine holds suspended matter such as yeast or fruit particles, this will settle naturally in a few days, perhaps helped by bottle rubbing as explained later. So wait, and don't filter. On the other hand a filter can be very useful if you are bottling lots of wine and have a great mass of yeast-sludge (lees) left in each fermentation vessel. These residues can be combined, roughly settled, and then filtered to make a bottle of ''plonk'' which otherwise would have been thrown away. Because of this blending process, ''plonk'' usually settles well and becomes very clear. Only buy a filter when you really need it.

On the other hand a funnel is absolutely essential. Glass or plastic are equally good, although plastic is better through being less fragile. Another advantage of a plastic funnel is that you can cut the neck so that it protrudes a sufficient length (say 1½ inches) into the neck of a wine bottle. The bottom of the funnel spout can be used as a guide for accurate bottle filling, as it will show the correct headspace necessary for efficient corking.

Hydrometers are made of plastic or glass. Both types are fragile, so be prepared to spend money on replacements. A point to check with glass ones after use is the base of the heavy part. A piece of the glass can easily come away and might not be noticed for some time. Its loss will not affect the wine being tested, but the instrument will give a misleading reading of specific gravity. Any tall clear jar can be used to hold the wine sample under test, as long as it can take the full length of the hydrometer. Plastic jars may not be transparent enough to let you have a clear view of the tiny scale on the hydrometer. A chemist's measuring cylinder or a small spagghetti storage jar are equally suitable, as long as they can be cleaned reliably (the bottle brush again).

Syphons come in various forms. The simplest and cheapest is a glass tube with a turned-over end, attached to a rubber tube. To start the siphon, you suck at the rubber tube to draw wine up the glass tube and as far as your mouth. With a dexterous movement you remove the rubber tube from your mouth, pinching it to prevent the wine from sinking down again, and put the rubber tube into the receiving vessel. In any siphoning operation the receiver has to be lower than the vessel being emptied, as no liquid will run uphill under gravity. This equipment is not recommended because it is basically unhygienic, also because the rubber tube cannot be reliably cleaned or be seen to be clean, but mainly because fresh wine does not taste all that good and is usually so potent that one's dexterity disappears very quickly during a long session.

Really it is altogether better to use an automatic siphon, which is all of plastic and which has a built-in squeeze pump. This syphon can be cleaned quite well by operating it in warm water a few times, using diluted household bleach as necessary to remove superficial staining. Don't forget to remove the bottom spacer plug when draining and drying-out: replace it again.

You might be tempted to buy a gadget for driving corks in. Succumb – there is no manual substitute if correctly-sized corks are to be driven home satisfactorily. There are various types; follow the instructions. If corks have been softened properly (see later) you can operate the gadget with a blow or your opened hand, and will not need to use a mallet. Plastic-covered wire of the sort used for bell- or lamp-wiring is very useful when driving corks in. Use a single short length which is hung to a depth of about two inches inside the bottle's neck. Then drive the cork in, when the air trapped by the descending cork can escape through the gap left between the neck and the wire. When the cork is fully home, withdraw the wire gently and the soft cork will swell out to fill the gap. There will be no surplus pressure left under the cork to drive it out later during storage. After a few uses you will have to use a fresh length of wire as the plastic insulation tends to crack and there is the risk of pulling it completely away, leaving the copper wire hanging in the wine and trapped by the cork. If this happens, draw the cork out and start again with a fresh cork and new

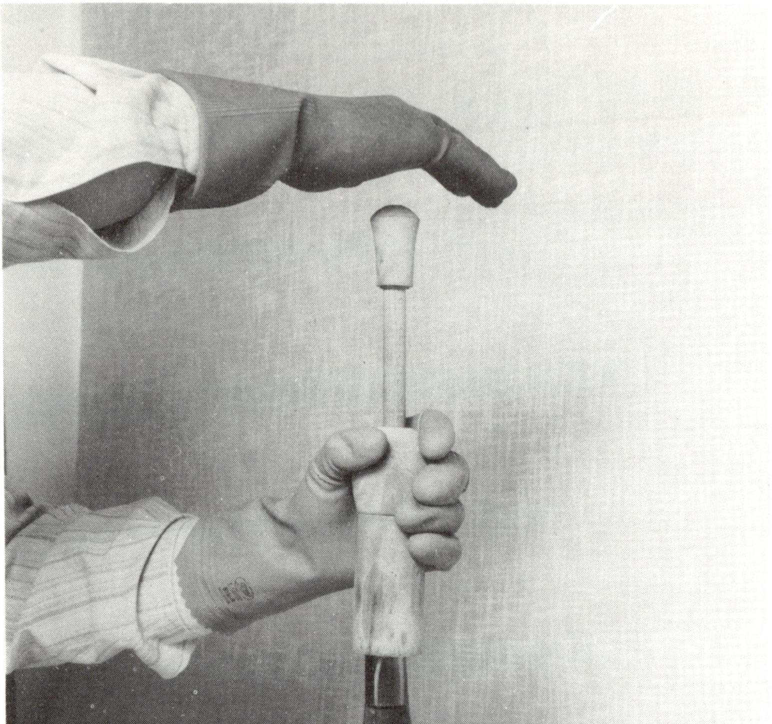

Driving a cork home: note the length of wire to release the air pressure.

wire. The copper wire will not hurt the wine, but possibly could make it unwholesome if left there, although I have not checked this point.

Special tools are available for rolling aluminium foil caps over the corked bottle neck. I have one but rejected it after a couple of attempts to use it, finding that a hand wiped round and down the foil is just as satisfactory. When using these foil caps, wipe the bottle neck with a damp cloth immediately beforehand: this cleans off wet cork extracts and helps the foil to conform to the neck shape and provides a secure seal against later mould attack.

Cleaning techniques

Wash hands well before starting wine making operations. Remember that the self-sterilising processes found in high temperature cooking are absent from wine making, which should be considered as akin to dairying. Whatever dissolves in the liquids, is left on the fruit or is otherwise added, will be left in the wine for you to drink, unless it settles with the yeast, so be clean, clean, CLEAN. Rubber gloves are useful for some operations like bottle washing and handling corks taken from boiling water. Keep special gloves for wine making and choose rough-surfaced ones which are good for gripping glass. However, if you wear gloves in hot water for too long, your hands will perspire, softening and detaching any flock lining present, and leading to peculiar odours. I find that clean, bare hands are best for most jobs as long as the skin is unbroken.

Clean bottles and demijohns with warm water and a little washing-up liquid; hot water in a sink and rubber gloves are best. Do not wash bottles in a bowl as this will only hold one bottle at a time. It is better to keep six or more bottles in the water so that five are soaking whilst one is being washed. Use a bottle brush for the insides, and a cloth for the outside. Roughly drain each washed bottle and lay it on its side on the draining board, with the neck downhill. When the board is full, pick each bottle up very carefully and gently pour out the drainings without twisting or shaking. This leaves very little residual detergent in the bottle, so reducing the number of rinsings needed. Then rinse the bottle several times under a gently-running cold water tap, giving three further rinsings when all the foam has disappeared. It is more efficient in time, use of water and in overall effectiveness to use a small amount of water for each rinse; about two tablespoons each time is enough. When all the bottles in a batch are washed (and there may be 36 of them) allow a final horizontal draining period and stand the bottles upright ready for filling.

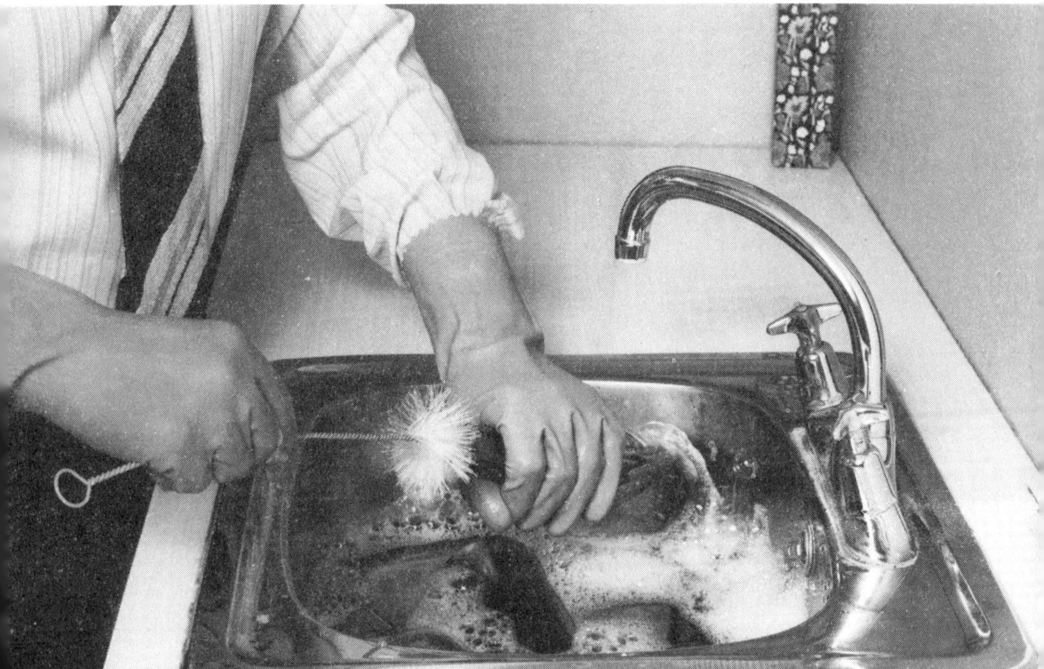

Cleaning bottles with a brush.

Bottles with dried-out wine residues in them can be cleaned by putting a tablespoon of ordinary sand in them and also a little water. This forms an abrasive which on shaking should do the trick. If this does not work completely, use a half-and-half mixture of household bleach and water. If this has not done the trick after overnight standing, throw the bottle away and resolve that in future you will rinse out an emptied wine bottle *before* it can dry out! In any event it is good practice to wash empty bottles properly before storing them away, and then to wash them up again immediately before a bottling session. Tell your friends the same.

When washing difficult items like airlocks, and inaccessible parts of fermentation tanks, use diluted household bleach. About two cups full in five gallons of water, stood overnight, will remove most soil from a tank. Any residue, if left after thorough rinsing, will not affect later batches of wine. Once it has worked, bleach converts into oxygen and common salt, which are of course harmless. Bleach itself is poisonous and corrosive when at full strength, but is pretty harmless if used as suggested, and rinses away easily.

Practise rinsing. Make a weak solution of any food dye, put into a clear white wine bottle, and check how many changes of clean rinsing water are needed to remove all visible colour. Proper rinsing then demands three additional rinses with more water after this. Try this technique with your other vessels. It is much more effective to use very small amounts of water, and give say ten rinses, than to use the same total volume of water in, say, three rinses.

Books tell you to sterilise everything with bisulphite solution. This may be fine for killing most yeasts and perhaps some bacteria, but if it is not thoroughly rinsed away afterwards (and this is difficult to check with a colourless chemical which bleaches food dyes), the residual bisulphite may kill or damage the yeast at the start of the fermentation. Again, such residues of the chemical could give a sulphurous taste to the wine and may change its colour. Even if you *do* rinse all the bisulphite away completely, then you are doing so with that same clean, but non-sterile, water which you would use anyway to wash up the vessel. So, don't use bisulphite.

When equipment has been cleaned, store it away properly, or else use it at once. Never closely stopper a wet container for storage, or musty smells will develop. For storage, let it pick up dust as it will (or store it neck down), and wash it up again immediately before use.

It is a good technique alternatively to plug a demijohn neck with a loosely folded paper towel for storage.

Materials and ingredients you need

SUGAR

You will almost always have to add sugar to your fermentations to achieve the correct final alcohol content. Household granulated sugar is satisfactory, even though it has to be chemically transformed in the "must" (by natural processes) before the yeast can consume it. Some recipes call for brown sugar or honey – the additional flavour so conferred to the wine may be worth the additional cost if you are a purist, but often cannot be noticed.

YEAST

You *can* use baker's yeast, but this means buying it especially for each brew. Better to buy wine maker's dried yeast. This comes in small plastic bags inside cartons, or in aluminium/polythene sachets. Although the sachets are often labelled for the type of wine which they should be used to make, e.g. claret or chablis, only the purist probably can detect the difference with normal dessert wines. Specialist yeasts are really only necessary for champagne, port or sherry. General-purpose yeast is quite suitable and for most wines is somewhat cheaper. Note that once a pack of yeast is opened, it will begin to deteriorate. Try to use it up within two months, as afterwards it may not be sufficiently active to start a fermentation off. So don't buy large quantities in a drum pack unless you are making wine all the time (as you should be); sachets are best for the occasional maker, purchased little and often.

YEAST NUTRIENT

This is a white, damp, crystalline material supplied in bulk in a bottle, or as tablets. The crystals are cheaper but tablets are easier to use. However, great accuracy in dispensing is not necessary, as long as you don't overdo it. Nutrient is already added to some brands of dried yeast, so check the packet before buying. Nutrient is often added to the concentrated juice in wine kits; it must always be added by you when making wine from fruit.

SODIUM BISULPHITE/CAMPDEN TABLETS

The former is supplied in bottles as a white powder, and the books tell you to use a solution of it to ''sterilise'' all your equipment. Don't bother; washing-up liquid and plenty of clean water will do the job just as well, as explained earlier. Bisulphite which has been diluted with an inert but soluble powder, and compressed into accurately defined doses, is marketed as ''Campden'' tablets. It is vital to use these for killing off moribund yeast cells at the end of fermentation. Always use the tablets to take advantage of the measured dose, which is usually 50 milligrams. It is unlikely that you could guess or weigh 50 milligrams of the powdered bisulphite, and the dosage to use is critical; too little and the yeast is not fully killed; too much and the wine will taste and smell of sulphur. and will need the services of a real chemist and his laboratory to remove it.

TANNIN

Tannin is a necessary addition to some fruit wines. It is not possible to guess when tannin is needed; follow what the recipe says. Don't use too much. Tannin is easiest to use in the liquid form and keeps for years.

ACIDS

Citric, tartaric or malic acid are called for in some recipes. For a start, do not be paranoic about the term ''acid''. People tend to think of all acids as terribly corrosive and deadly poisonous at all concentrations, yet will put lemon juice on their pancakes, or vinegar on their chips, without a thought! Common experience shows that water-soluble acids such as vinegar can be easily and completely rinsed away with water. So let's have no more concern about acids used in wine making – they are just powdered ingredients with a sharp taste.

Acids are used in wine making to ''balance'' the ''must'' so that the yeast has the best possible environment in which to live and do its job. You will not know what that optimum acidity should be for your particular yeast, and would not be able to measure it if you did. So just add the amount and type of acid called for in the recipe, remembering that the more acid is added, the sharper in taste the wine will be.

CORKS

Use good quality straight (parallel sided) corks about one and a quarter inches long. Corks with an integrally-shaped flat top, or with a plastic cap, have a shorter length available to make the seal, and are unsuitable for long-term wine storage. However, these particular corks are quite useful as temporary closures when a bottle is not being emptied in one session, and needs saving for another day. Also available are hollow stoppers made of plastic. These are relatively cheap but in time tend to creep upwards out of the bottle neck, and so are useless. They can of course be inserted easily without prior soaking, so amateurs are beguiled into buying them. Better to purchase the best corks available from your supplier.

Types of capsules, corks and stoppers.

BOTTLE CAPS

These are available as thin aluminium foil preforms which can be closed down over the neck by a wiping action of the hand. Another, more expensive type is a preformed plastic cap which is quite thick and which offers better mechanical protection than the metal foil ones. These plastic caps are shrunk on by the gradual action of moisture. Whichever type you choose, they are essential when full wine bottles are stored on their sides, especially in damp conditions, as moulds will tend to grow on the corks, kept damp by wine diffusion, and will be unappetising, to say the least. The plastic covers are quite tough but correspondingly harder to remove, while the metal foil caps can be only too easy to remove as there is a danger of their catching in the small neck hole at the back of your horizontal wine storage rack, and thus being torn off as you withdraw the bottle. Mice also gnaw at the foil caps if bottles are stored under severe conditions, as for example in a garage. On balance, it seems that plastic caps are preferable; I must change over to them myself!

LABELS

If you can store your wine in a dry place under non-condensing conditions, and if you are certain to get no deposit in the wine on storage (this is a big *if*), then use fancy labels so your guests can see them when you serve the wine. To be more practical, if your wine is stored in a damp place, such labels will suffer from mould growth and will soon become unreadable. A reliable, albeit un-decorative, alternative is to use the common, small white self-adhesive labels which come on a backing release paper, and to write on them with a coarse graphite pencil of the kind that carpenters use. All inks, especially Biros, fade quite quickly in damp conditions, and moulds thrive on the glues used on labels except for this kind. Graphite pencil is always readable, even if you have to rub surplus dirt or mildew off it first.

Selecting Fruit

If you use kits, then fruit is not needed as all the grape content is contained in the concentrate supplied. In the absence of fresh fruit because of seasonal shortage, one can use canned fruit bought in bulk from a supermarket, or even cheap tinned jam. When using jam, you must allow for it containing around 65 per cent of sugar, so you will have to make some calculation of the amount of fruit actually in it, and make a corresponding reduction in the sugar to be added according to the recipe.

Remember that all wine must have an appreciable grape content to give it body and flavour. If you employ fresh grapes, which are expensive in money to purchase and expensive in effort to grow, be sure that they have not been sprayed with the wrong chemicals during their lifetime. In other words, if you are growing them and have to use sprays, take advice, read the labels on the bottles and make sure that suitable materials are used. Grapes which have ripened and then been left on the vine to the point of shrivelling and going mouldy are used deliberately to make some specialist German wines, and so can be perfectly well used by the amateur grower. However, in my experience, such wine, whilst as good as any other, does not seem to be especially distinctive.

Choose good quality fresh fruit of the kind you would eat for dessert; do not use seconds or sub-standard fruit, windfalls or the like, as enzymes are released on bruising which can affect the fermentation process. With good fruit, however, the riper it is, the more sugar it contains, and the less you need to add to make a "must".

Some recipes call for exotic ingredients such as tree sap or grape vine prunings. You must be desperately short of fruit or money to go to such lengths: I suggest that you avoid these unpromising materials until you have become a dedicated and esoteric wine buff.

Preparing the Fruit

Clean up hard-skinned fruit like apples and gooseberries by stirring them around in a sink full of water containing half a cupful of household bleach. Tepid water is best. Flies, wireworms, earwigs, bad or suspect fruit, leaves, twigs and odd scraps float to the top. Take out the washed fruit (wearing rubber gloves of course) and rinse it in cold water. Rinsing need not be *too* thorough as any surplus bleach soon gets converted to ordinary household salt, and is harmless.

Only wash fruit which has strong skins, like apples, plums and gooseberries, where individual items can easily be handled. Pick through soft fruits, raspberries, blackberries etc., taking out all insects and dirt, but use without washing as this can take away much of the flavour.

Mashing apples by means of a power drill and blade.

When soft fruit comes in bunches, such as blackcurrants and elderberries, roughly remove the fruit from the stalks using a table fork as a tool. Despite what some books say, it is not vital to remove all vestiges of the stalks; you will never notice any difference in the final taste. To crush the skins of most soft fruit, including grapes, and to release the juice, use a power drill fitted up with a paint stirrer paddle. This beats up the mass very powerfully, so that 10 pounds of grapes can be converted into a usable slime in about three minutes. An alternative way, better suited to smaller berries, is to wash your hands, then don rubber gloves and crush the fruit between the palms of your hands with a kind of washing action. The gloves, or your hands if you preferred to use them bare, can be decolourised afterwards with warm water and a very little household bleach.

Crush apples with a baulk of timber about three inches square, putting a few at a time in the bottom of a strong plastic bucket. Quickly transfer the fragments to your fermenting tank containing the requisite quantity of water, so that the apple does not turn too brown. As long as the apples are of good quality there is no need to core or skin them, as you will already have inspected each one and have cut out any bad portions at the washing stage. If you baulk at the crushing method, pass the apples through a potato chipper. In any event, the aim is to expose a large area of apple to the water in which it is steeped, so the flavour is fully extracted.

Some recipes call for ten pounds of apples to be extracted with water to make, ultimately, one gallon of wine. This is too much apple: in a normal rectangular fermentation tank one gallon of water will properly cover only six to seven pounds of apples. Any fragments in the tank but above the water line are a nuisance to stir around and their flavour is not properly extracted.

Grapes and other soft fruit can with advantage have their cells softened up by deep freezing and thawing before crushing. To get the flavour and fermentability out of fruit it is essential to break the skins. Grapes are best broken down in a bucket after pulling them off the stalks. Ten pounds of grapes at a time is a convenient amount.

Use the power drill and paint mixer paddle as suggested before. By getting the paddle in position just off the bottom, and near one side of the bucket, you will feel a strong pull downwards which indicates that useful skin-breaking work is going on. Hard, unripe grapes will

Crushing apples with a baulk of timber.

float to the top at the end of the process and can be ''popped'' between finger and thumb.

Rhubarb is best picked when fully ripe and as red as can be. Choose thick sticks as the juice and flavour can be extracted most easily from these. Then wash the sticks and deep freeze them for a few days; stand them upright in a bucket like a big bunch of flowers until they thaw, which will take a surprisingly long time. All the cell walls will have broken, leaving the sticks incredibly soft and floppy. Much of the juice will collect in the bucket anyway, but extract the rest by taking one stick at a time, laying it out straight in a long tray with raised edges, and rolling it from one end to the other with a rolling pin. Collect all the juice in the bucket and you are ready for the next stage. It might be tempting to try putting unfrozen sticks through a kitchen mincer; don't bother, because the ''strings'' get caught around the spiral, and the mincer must be dismantled after every other stick! Also, it is as well not to extract the juice and flavour with hot water, as this can also bring out too much oxalic acid, which is not good for you. Hot water also tends to make the wine unclearable later.

A good ploy is to make mixed, anonymous wine from the spare, surplus fruit which you may find during the annual clear-out of the freezer (assuming that you have one). Just take the juice out in any way which seems appropriate, and make a ''must'' based on a middle-of-the-road recipe. About three pounds of fruit is a good quantity, but don't forget the grape juice.

I have earlier made mention of jam as a source of fruit. Only bother if it seems to be significantly cheaper, or if your wife has had a kitchen disaster, bearing in mind the cost of sugar, which constitutes at least 65 per cent of it. On the other hand, you might be prepared to spend out on jam for a fruit which would otherwise be too expensive to buy, such as apricot, or just too tiresome to pick, such as blackcurrants or blackberries.

Do not use bisulphite or Campden solution to wash fruit. Unless you rinse the fruit very well, with the consequent risk of taking the flavour away, some residues of the chemical could remain and inhibit the first fermentation of the ''must''. I have never found that enzymes on the fruit surface have affected wine making.

Making a "Must"

The term "must" has been used several times already; I hope you knew what was meant. "Must" is the mixture of fruit pulp or juice, water, sugar, yeast and whatever else is needed to start and carry through the ferment. Your recipes will tell you how much of each ingredient to use per gallon of must, and the fruit is prepared as outlined in the previous section. In my opinion "must" *must* always contain some grape content, although others would not concur. Do not believe those old country practitioners who claim to make wine solely out of rose petals or parsnips. They will produce for your delectation a dry, strongly intoxicating drink, but this is not wine: grapes are essential to produce a round fruity flavour and a full body. It is the British wine-making reputation of using any old fruit which makes foreigners so leery of our efforts.

The "must" *must* be clean. Whatever is in it, except for fruit and yeast solids, you are ultimately going to drink. So be careful what you put in, and how you handle it.

Recipe books all present the theory of fermentation, so there is no point in my going all through it again, as this text presumes that you will have obtained a recipe book with basics from elsewhere. Suffice it to say that in the presence of water, and at an adequately mild temperature, natural processes convert sugar from the fruit, or the cane or beet sugar that you add, into chemically simpler sugars on which the yeast can feed. If yeast feeds on a sugary liquid with free access to the air, then carbon dioxide gas (the bubbles in sparkling wines), acids and water are formed. Carried out in a controlled manner, this produces high-grade vinegar. However, if air is excluded, (hence the closed fermentation vessel and the air-lock), then the yeast only reaches a half-way stage, producing carbon dioxide gas just the same, but also the alcohol you so much desire.

So, the "must" is handled in an enclosed atmosphere. As fermentation proceeds, the air in the tank is displaced upwards by the heavier carbon dioxide gas and all will be well. Any insects or other life which escaped your eagle eye during fruit preparation will be suffocated by this unbreathable gas. The presence of their bodies will have no detectable effect on the wine, except perhaps to give it a bit more body.

Having said all that it must be pointed out that some recipes require that a fruit pulp should be made up and kept (with or without added yeast) for up to two weeks in an open vessel. A completely open vessel is best avoided in my view, but admittedly it is sometimes easier to stir the contents of a big bucket than it is to thoroughly mix the contents of a five gallon tank. So, if the "must" is unprotected by an airlock for some time, such as the 1–2 weeks' soaking which can be needed to extract all the colour from dark grapes, cover it carefully with a lintless cloth and put a heavy board on the top to hold it down firmly all round the edge.

Alternatively use a baby-care type of bucket or a fermentation vessel with a snap-on lid, as long as you are satisfied that it is of food-grade plastic. If the Gods are against you, and the seal is not too good, the smell of the yeast will not only repel your family and friends, but will attract Drusophila (known commonly as fruit- or vinegar-flies) which might land in the must. These flies have biological materials called enzymes on their wings which hasten conversion of sugar to vinegar, so that any small contamination could lead to odd flavours in your final product.

If you grow grapes, a good plan is to make as much pure grape wine as you can from the undiluted juice. Add no water at all, but add sufficient sugar to obtain the correct final alcohol content. At this point it might be worth reminding you that a white table wine should contain about 11% of alcohol, and a red dessert wine could go up to about 15%. Try to make your home-made wines on the strong side, as it is no use going to all that trouble and expense to bottle what otherwise would be largely water. If the wine seems too strong and you are thirsty, you could (but perish the thought) add a little water.

When wine is made with fruit other than grapes, always include concentrated grape juice, red, white or rosé as appropriate, as one of the ingredients. Add half as much concentrate as you would in a purely "kit" must, and use the chosen fruit in the usual way. Thus do you add the essential grapiness to the wine, and achieve that satisfying thickness and body which good wines have.

If you feel in an expansive (and incidentally expensive) mood, use raisins or sultanas as the grape content. Remember however that each individual skin must be broken, by a knife-cut or by using a kitchen chopper, for them to be fermentable. The operation is time-consuming and messy.

Certain fruits, notably apples and plums, contain pectin. This will make the wine cloudy, with no other discernible effect, but cannot in any way be filtered out at any stage of the process. A white powder named "pectolytic enzyme" is used in the must before adding yeast, to digest the pectin. The maker's instructions tell you to add it when the basic must is prepared, and to allow a day for it to work before adding the yeast. I have never ever found this to be sufficient length of time, whether when using powdered or liquid versions of the enzyme. Allow two days at least, keeping the must in a warm place; even then the final wine may be somewhat cloudy. A test for pectin was described earlier in the section on "Equipment you need".

When making up the must, keep details on a sheet of paper. Some people keep a full-scale log book and can then refer to past successes and failures. Others like me keep just a small sheet of paper which can be tucked into the ring handle of a demijohn, or under the handle of a five gallon fermentation tank. Note on the record an easy reference to the recipe you are using, (such as a book page number), the date of starting and, particularly, the amount to be made. It helps to list the ingredients as added, especially if some are added on one day, such as when fruit is extracted with hot water, and the rest are added later. Take care to record the initial specific gravity, as this is the value on which all your subsequent calculations are based. As fermentation proceeds, you will check specific gravity from time to time, and write down the result and the date. You will soon get a feel for how fast your fermentation normally proceed, and this will be helpful experience if the fermentations should ever "stick".

Fermentation speed is not constant. My own fermentations normally go pretty fast; very often a kit fermentation will be completely over in 10–14 days, and my fruit fermentations rarely last more than a month. Other people find that their processes take much longer, and two to four months is not unknown. There is no great virtue in fermentations being extra fast or slow, but it is useful for you to have an idea of your particular yeast work rate, as this can alert you to impending trouble with stuck fermentations or with anaerobic conditions.

Many recipes say that you should set up a "starter bottle" as an aid to make the must start fermenting. A starter is a mini-fermentation. In goes water, a little sugar, nutrient and some yeast. Kept warm, the yeast gets going in a few hours and is then added to the main must mix, which begins fermenting almost right away. In practice, however, provided your yeast is reasonably fresh, the simple addition of it in dried powder form to the must is enough to get things going anyway in two to three days. This is not a long enough wait for things to go wrong with the must. However, if fermentation does not begin after three days, it would be wise to invoke the starter bottle method. The materials used in the starter mix have no influence on quantities used for the must.

You may, at some time, sense that the must is just not going to begin proper fermentation, and feel that in some way the yeast reacts as if it has been poisoned. At other times, a fermentation will go just so far and then stop. In such cases, proceed as follows. Get a starter mix going really actively, and transfer it to a one gallon fermentation vessel. Add to it about half a pint of the inactive must, set in a warm place and await events. After a slow start, the half pint and starter should begin fermenting. When this happens, and not too soon, add a further half pint of the stuck must to the now-active brew. As the amount of actively fermenting must increases, you can add more and more of the stuck must, but always ensure that its volume is less than that which is actively working. This is a useful way of dealing with a must which has been poisoned, for example by accidental addition of too much bisulphite.

Keep the must in a warm place; whether in the light or dark is immaterial. A clothes airing cupboard is quite good especially if a particular fermentation is going too slowly, but on the other hand any excess of warmth can lead to very violent fermentation at first, especially with clarets. The fast rush of carbon dioxide can sweep out the contents of the air-lock, and even the stopper itself, with decorative effects on any adjacent stored linen. I was banned from our airing cupboard very early in the game!

A windowsill in the sun can be a good place as the vessel is protected from most chance of accidents, but can become very cold at night and the jar should be opaque, covered, or shielded from too much direct light. To overcome all temperature problems, a wine heater might be used, but can occasionally pose its own set of problems should the thermostat decide to stick in the "on" position. Most modern wine heaters are, however, very reliable.

Obviously, if the must is kept too cool, the time to complete the fermentation will increase.

During Fermentation

As fermentation proceeds, more and more yeast cells form, so the must becomes very cloudy. In due course, cells die and settle to the bottom to form a buff coloured layer. During the first few days it helps to shake the fermentation tank well to keep the yeast in circulation. If the tank is a plastic one, lifting it will draw air in through the airlock. Be sure the water in the lock is clean. Later, as the wine ferments towards the end, it is better to let the spent yeast settle out.

If you want to make a really dry wine, ferment out all the sugar, at which point bubbles no longer leave the airlock and the spent yeast starts to settle out naturally. Leave it for two to four days until much of the yeast has settled, then rack the wine (see the next section for some details). Then add Campden solution to the racked wine.

First time wine drinkers tend to like sweet wine at a specific gravity (S.G.) of about 1.010: as your taste changes you may go for drier wines with a lower S.G. down to 0.995. The hydrometer must be used freely to check progress of the fermentation so that you can stop it at the proper point. Normally a must is brought to an S.G. of 1.080 with sugar at the start of a fermentation, as this is near the maximum concentration which new yeast can stand. Middle-of-the-road dryish wine has an S.G. of about 1.006, while a sweet one has a S.G. of 1.010 and a very dry one is down to 0.996.

The hydrometer indicates the specific gravity (S.G.) of a liquid, which is the weight of a volume of liquid compared with the weight of an equal volume of water. In our case, the liquid of interest is the must, at the time when it is ready to be fermented. The S.G. value allows an estimate to be made of the sugar content of the liquid, and of the final alcohol content which will result when all the sugar is transformed by the yeast. The Table shows how much sugar to add, to supplement that already in the fruit, in order to reach the required alcohol content in the finished wine.

Other dissolved materials, apart from sugar, can increase the S.G. of the must. The amounts of these are normally insignificant for practical purposes, but are enough to prevent the hydrometer from being a totally accurate instrument. However, it provides sufficiently useful indications to allow adequate control of the process of wine making. After all, no-one will worry if their white wine has 11.13 per cent of alcohol when the maker hoped it would be 11.15 per cent!

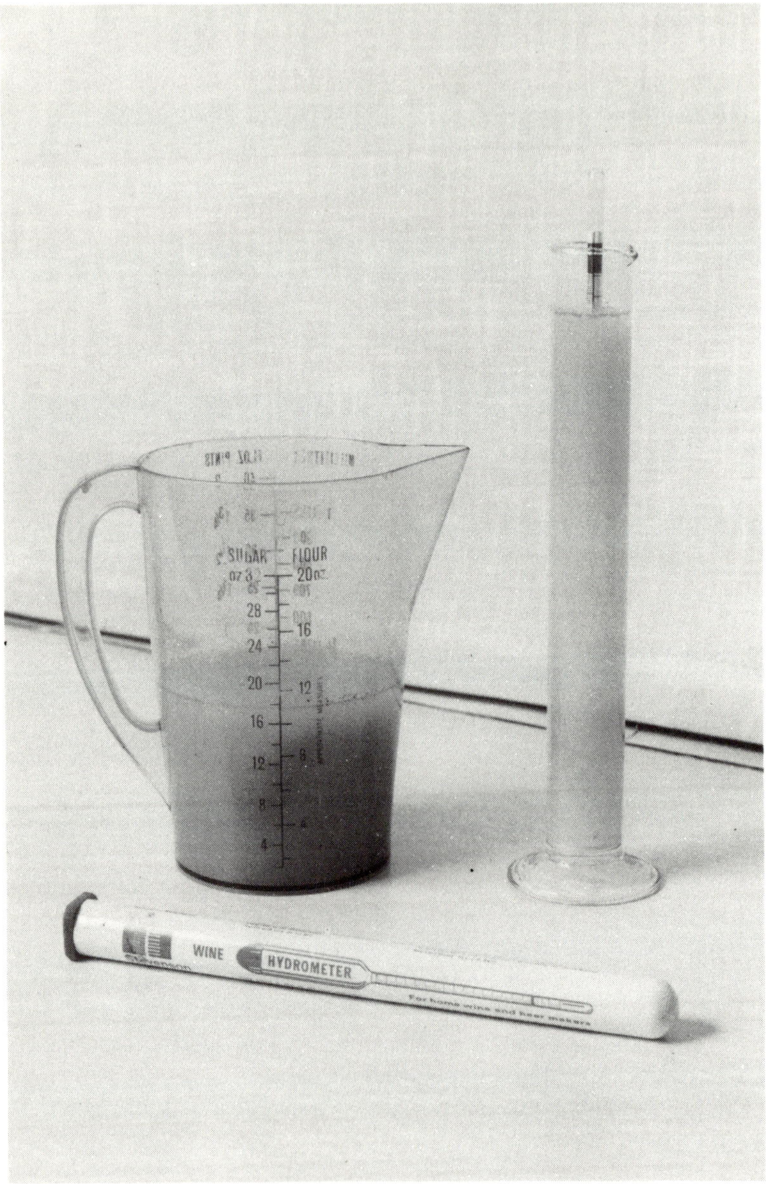

Hydrometer and jar.

In practice, and with practice, one comes to think in terms of the last two figures of the S.G. reading. Thus a normal must for a white wine will have enough sugar in it to show an S.G. of 1.080, that is, 80 points. As the number of points goes down, so too does the sugar content, while the alcohol content rises correspondingly. Thus at 12 points (S.G. 1.012), we have a sweet wine, which becomes medium-dry at 06 points, and very dry at −5 points (S.G. 0.995).

Hydrometer reading	*Quantity of sugar in each gallon of must*		*Percentage of alcohol (by volume) which that sugar will produce.*
	lb.	oz.	
1.010		2	0.9
1.015		4	1.6
1.020		7	2.3
1.025		9	3.0
1.030		12	3.7
1.035		15	4.4
1.040	1	1	5.1
1.045	1	3	5.8
1.050	1	5	6.5
1.055	1	7	7.2
1.060	1	9	7.8
1.065	1	11	8.6
1.070	1	13	9.2
1.075	1	15	9.9
1.080	2	1	10.6
1.085	2	4	11.3
1.090	2	6	12.0
1.095	2	8	12.7
1.100	2	10	13.4
1.105	2	12	14.1
1.110	2	14	14.9

Interpolations can be made between all these pairs of figures where intermediate S.G. readings or amounts are involved. If you are making more than 1 gallon of must, multiply up the quantities of sugar to be added. Remember that the S.G. is a property of the liquid itself, and is independent of the volume you are dealing with.

Suppose you do start with a must at S.G. 1.080, and you want it to ferment until the wine has a S.G. of 1.002, which is a fairly dry drink. How is this control achieved? If just left to go its own way, the yeast will eat all the sugar it can until the final S.G. is 0.995. This is more dry than you want. What you have to do is to check the S.G. frequently with the hydrometer, and check how the value gradually approaches the desired one. If you wish to appear scientific in approach, plot a little graph for the process, showing days since the start of fermentation on the horizontal axis, and S.G. on the vertical axis. Plotting a daily S.G. reading on this graph will soon give a curved line which will help you predict the day when the S.G. will be correct. Do not of course rely only on the prediction; check the S.G. by hydrometer near the end of the fermentation. If you are absent and the fermentation inadvertently goes on too long so that the S.G. gets too low, do not despair. Knowing the amount of wine you have to deal with, the density/sugar concentration tables already given will enable you to calculate how much granulated sugar to add to the over-dry wine to return it to your specified S.G. value. This commercial sugar does not have the same quality of sweetness as the yeast-modified sugar which normally flavours wine, but you will never notice if the quantity added is small.

If it looks as though you will never get as far as all this, because the must does not seem to want to begin fermenting after two to three days from adding the yeast, then add more yeast from a freshly opened packet, or try a starter bottle as described earlier.

Mention was made of the fact that yeast can only take so much sugar at a time, being inhibited by too rich a diet. If you want a really strong wine then a lot of sugar must ultimately be added. In this case it would be better to divide the total of sugar to be added into two or three lots, letting the most active fermentation from one lot subside before adding the next sugar instalment. Such kindness will help the yeast to flourish and do its job better, especially if it starts off a little weak or old. Always keep a note of all the sugar which has been added, so that you will have some idea how strong the final product will be.

The "must" might "stick". This means that fermentation might never start, or that it might go so far and then obstinately stop, apparently for good. Wines stick for a variety of reasons, all connected with the conditions not being good for yeast reproduction. For example, each yeast needs a not-too-wide range of acidity in the "must" for it to grow well. The recipe will state how much acid should have been added, but selection of unripe fruit may add enough extra acidity to send conditions over the top. If in doubt, take a little of the stuck "must" and add a large pinch of bicarbonate of soda: if it fizzes, the acid level is perhaps too high. Controlled addition of more might get the fermentation going again without ultimate detriment to the wine. If the "must" continues to stick, try gradually adding it to a thriving starter as described before.

Eventually fermentation will have reached the point at which you wish the yeast would go away and stop converting sugar, so you can get on with the next stage. This is done by adding one or more Campden tablets, which kill the yeast cells in a matter of minutes.

Demijohn, bubbler and record sheet

The dead cells settle noticeably in a few hours; you will see an ever-decreasing layer of cloudy wine covering a buff coloured sediment. A great joy (as it happens) is to observe the top layer of almost clear wine, which becomes deeper and deeper as the days go on. If the wine is from apple or plum, and the top layer stays quite cloudy, then there may be a pectin problem, which suggests that you did not give the pectolytic enzyme long enough to do its work right at the beginning. However, it is too late now to do anything more with the enzyme – we must read on and see later what to do.

One Campden tablet per gallon is sufficient for white wine, two tablets for reds. The tablets are very hard, and do not dissolve easily even in hot water, so are best crushed between two nesting teaspoons before dissolving in hot water. Hot water will lead to the release of sulphur fumes: their loss at this stage does not seem to impair their efficiency as a yeast killer, but will not help the inside of your lungs. Don't breathe the fumes. The small amount of water needed to dissolve the tablets will not materially affect your wine volume calculations.

Adding Campden solution to red wine will bleach the colour somewhat, but it will return to normal in a short time. Do not add too many Campden tablets as they will leave a "sulphur" flavour which is unlikely to go in the maturing stage.

Settling and Clarifying

Use of Campden tablets will leave you with finished, but immature, wine which is contaminated with dead yeast cells. These will settle to the bottom over a period of days. Do not be tempted to leave this situation unchanged for more than two weeks. Even if the wine is not clear by then (and often it is not), rack (siphon) off the wine and keep the sediment (lees) separately – a spare wine bottle with a temporary cork will do quite well. If lees is left in contact with the wine for too long, bacterial action might get going and make the wine smell and taste of bad eggs. This can be overcome, but is of course best avoided.

As with all other manipulations involving transferring wine, the strong, though pleasant, smell can attract fruit flies. Be sure they do not get into the wine and achieve this either by careful exclusion or by swatting them. Do not risk using insect sprays near the wine.

"Racking" is a term which we have just begun using. This means removing the clear liquid and so separating it from the lees. It is quite possible to do this by careful pouring, or "decanting" as the chemist calls it, provided the vessel is not so heavy that you cannot support it for a sufficient time. Take care to tilt the vessel slowly, gently and steadily – no vibration or you will stir up the sediment. An alternative method which takes away all the physical effort, but which requires that the vessel be translucent if not actually transparent, is to use a siphon. You must be able to see that the bottom end of the siphon tube is just above the top of the layer of lees, otherwise you will certainly suck some dead yeast cells into what would otherwise be clear wine. Racking is best done using quite a large vessel as a receiver; a one gallon jar is quite good, although a three pint jug can also be pressed into service. It is altogether too fiddly and messy to try racking directly into wine bottles. Whatever happens, make sure of course that the receiver is very clean and can be sealed reasonably well in the short term against ingress of air and insects. If you are racking several batches of wine in one session, try "leapfrogging" the receivers. Rack settled wine from tank A into tank B, then put the lees from A into a spare wine bottle and swill A out with a little clean water (note the oily appearance as your wine "sees" fresh water). Then use tank A as the receiver when racking out tank C. You can see that with this method you only need one initially empty tank, no matter how many tanks of wine are to be racked. This method avoids formal washing up, as vessels wet with diluted wine are as clean as you are likely to get.

Using plastic fermentation tanks made of polythene or other translucent material might seem to pose a problem in seeing whether the wine has settled properly and adequately clear. Not so; just look downwards into the neck and observe whether you can see the top of the layer of lees. If you can, the wine is ready for racking.

You may find that the wine as first racked is not as clear as you would like (star-bright is a term often used, and is usually applicable to commercial wines). So watch it. If in a few days some more sediment comes down, judge when this is complete and then rack again. Each time you rack, of course, there remains yet more lees and always some cloudy wine which the siphon could not take up. No matter; put these residues in a spare wine bottle and you will be able to process the mixture into a passable "plonk", with very little actual waste. The value of large scale operations now becomes apparent. If you had only a gallon to start with, then after a few rackings you could be almost one bottle short.

A useful pump siphon.

Your wine may be now be very clear, in which case be thankful and bottle it. If it is not quite clear, leave some to stand in a white wine bottle and watch it for a few days, making sure that the main bulk of the wine is protected from the air and the dreaded fruit fly while you await events. It may happen that further slow settlement occurs, in which case you must make a judgement about how long to leave it all before you bottle and whether you are prepared otherwise to get it out of the way by bottling and accept that sediment will appear in the bottle in its own good time. I tend always to bottle rather early, in the interests of getting the wine away from the air as soon as possible, and so almost always have some sediment appearing.

If your wine does not noticeably clear any more on standing for a few more days, test it for the presence of starch or pectin, using the iodine or methylated spirit tests detailed in the ''Equipment'' section, but do not of course taste or keep the wine which you have tested. If starch or pectin are present you will not be able to filter them out with normal wine filtering equipment, although you will not believe it and will have to try nonetheless, as I often do even after all these years!

A pectin haze can sometimes be miraculously cleared by storing the wine in a glass demijohn in a warm, dry, place and then rubbing the jar surface briskly. Try at different times rubbing with flannel, wool, nylon, silk and even with clean, dry hands. This treatment has been known to work: I think that static electricity is generated by the rubbing, and this neutralises the electric charges which stabilises the haze. If it works, the haziness settles neatly and promptly in a couple of days.

If this arcane art does not work, you are left with at least two options, which are:

1. Blend this cloudy wine with some other cloudy wine made from a different type of fruit. Sometimes the two clouds interact, settling readily and leaving clear wine above. Naturally you will experiment with a little of each wine first, mixing in the ubiquitous clear wine bottle, in case the two wines do *not* react in this convenient way. A disadvantage of this method is that it presupposed that you frequently make intractable wine, which I hope is not the case, and another is that you lose the character of each of the fruit wines you so carefully tried to make. Whilst it is true that wine should not taste just like the fruit it was made from, all the same if you make plum wine it is nice to be able to say that is what it *is*.

Using a commercial filter

2. Bottle the wine anyway, and hope that storage for a year or more will work the miracle. I often resort to this method and it is surprising how frequently it works. If the bottles are stored on their sides during maturation, the cloudiness which is trying to settle has less distance to fall before it hits the wall of the bottle and also the precipitate which has already collected. When cloudy particles touch, they usually tend to coagulate and will not afterwards separate so readily; this means you have a real chance of decanting the wine in a clear condition. But only if the bottle is handled carefully – see later notes on serving. Note that the sediment is not in any way harmful to the health, only to your aesthetic sensibility.

You may notice that I have not enthused over filtering, although fully aware that very technical-looking filter apparatus is available in the shops. In my experience, any suspended matter in wine which would filter out satisfactorily is coarse enough to settle out under the effect of gravity alone in a few days. The filtration process tends to expose the wine to the air for rather a long time, and this in turn can lead to loss of some of the essential flavouring matter, and possibly oxidation, and certainly encourages the return of the dreaded Drusophila. Filter paper which is fine enough to hold back all the sediment and to make the wine star-bright is very reluctant to let the wine pass through, and clogs up very easily, so you often have to pour the funnel-full of wine back in the storage vessel and start again with a fresh paper. If you use a looser weave of paper, then the wine will pour through easily and be apparently unchanged. If you use the inert powder filter aid, this can be quite good, but soon tends to clog up the pores of the cloth filter bag which has to be used. This then involves you in squeezing the bag rather like a cow's udder in order to restore the flow. At the end you may have clear wine, but you certainly also have a bag full of dreadfully coloured and disgusting slime which must be disposed of. The bag must be very thoroughly cleaned if it is to be of any use next time.

Filtration is a lot of boring work – try to avoid it!

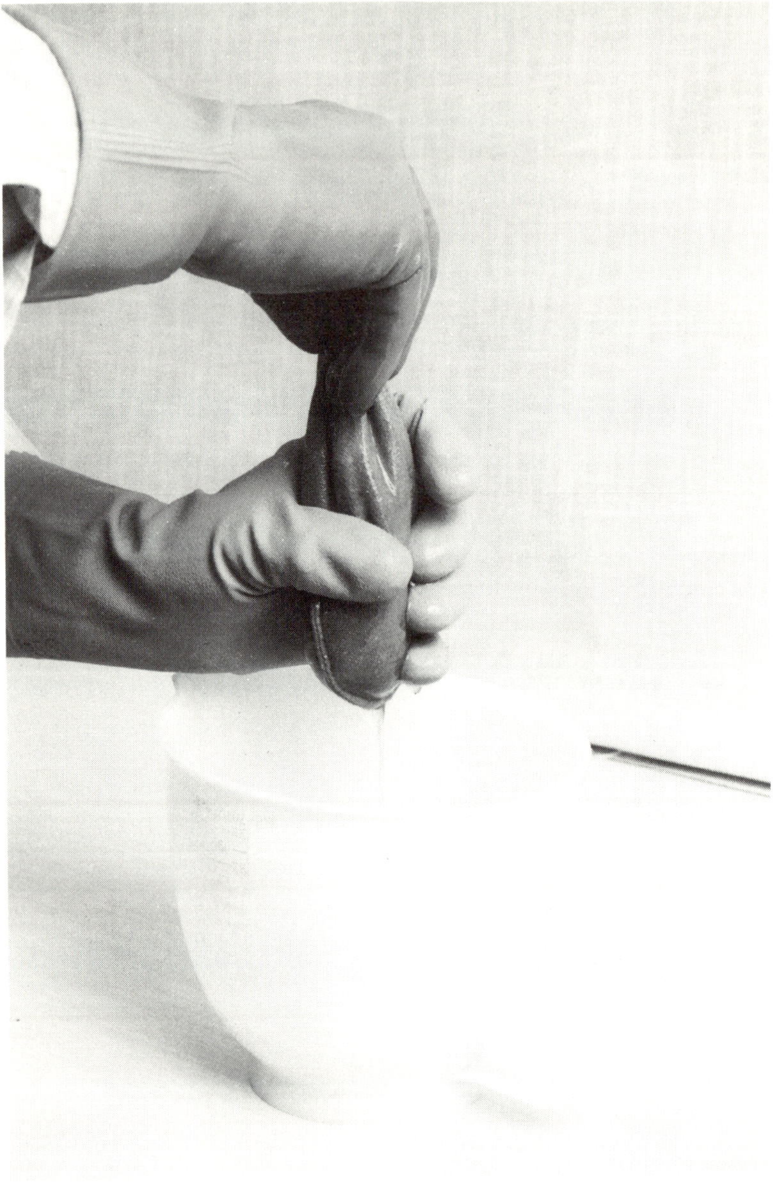

Squeezing a filter bag

The bottling process

The tedious part is washing the bottles really well and then draining them thoroughly. Use a plastic funnel to guide the wine into the bottle necks. You will spill enough anyway, without trying to be clever and fill direct from a jug or demijohn. Cut the funnel stem to such a length that when it is put in the bottle, the bottom of the stem is at the point up to which you must fill.

Watch out for the fruit-fly. If one falls into a full bottle of wine fill it up to the very top with wine and hook out the corpse with your clean finger, then pour out the surplus wine and cork in the ordinary way. Pray that the wine will not go bad on maturing, but mark the label with a sign to remind you to be ready for a poor result when you open the bottle in time to come. Then if this bottle is not acceptable, it will not mislead you into thinking that the whole batch is bad.

If filled, but uncorked bottles are to be left for more than a few minutes, push them all together into a compact group and cover the serried ranks of necks with a soft teatowel. Never be tempted to leave them uncorked overnight; it is much better to stay up late, finish the job, and then feel virtuous all next day.

Wine-making books tell you to soften corks by immersing them in water for 24 hours. They are to be held under the surface by pressing them down with a weight such as a tea plate. A much better way is to put enough water in an electric kettle to cover the element, add the correct number of corks (count your bottles) and bring the water to the boil. With the kettle switched off, you can pick out each cork safely with a rubber-gloved hand, or with cooking tongs, and will at the same time find three things:

1. The cork is of just the correct softness to drive into the bottle.
2. The cork is effectively sterile.
3. You have saved 23 hours and 58 minutes!

If you use a corking machine to drive corks into the bottle neck, and it is difficult to do it otherwise, the air trapped between the wine and the descending cork will tend to push the softened cork out again, to the detriment of final appearance and the effective fit of the foil cap. Avoid the problem with a few inches of electrical wire, which has a centre of copper wire and an outer layer of plastic insulation. Loop the wire into an inverted "U" bend and drop one limb of the "U" into the bottle neck, with the other limb hanging outside. Drive in the cork

Softening corks.

and listen for the hiss as all that compressed air escapes past the obstruction. Then withdraw the wire with a smooth and strong action, when the cork will swell out to fill the gap. In this way the corks will always finish up about one tenth of an inch below the rim of the neck, which is the best situation. Unless, of course, you have cut the stem of the plastic funnel too short in the first place, in which case you will, if using it as a marker, have overfilled the bottle, with severe risk of breakage as the cork is driven home. The "head-space" of air between the wine and cork should be about ½ inch.

Commercial wine companies mature the wine for months in vats before bottling, so the product as marketed is always star-bright. You too may choose to store the wine in bulk in one, five or ten gallon lots as the wine books say you should. This depends however, on:

1. Whether you have a sufficient capacity of suitable containers. Remember that they should be made of glass, as plastic is liable to allow ingress of oxygen into the wine and may generate unpleasant flavours which dissolve out into it.

2. Whether your safe storage area is better fitted to hold big tanks or rows of bottles.

The only alternative to maturing in bulk is to bottle while the wine is yet young. The penalty for doing this is that sediment will almost certainly come down as maturing proceeds, (a good reason for not filtering unnecessarily when preparing a bottle) and this must be recognised when presenting the bottle later.

Mention was made earlier of putting the lees, which was left after racking the wine, on to one side in a clear wine bottle. Leave these to settle out for 2–3 days, and you will be surprised how much almost clear wine collects above the more compacted sludge. This top liquid is a good candidate for filtering, or it can be blended with other wine to make it really clear. The result may be "plonk", but after maturing it will be just as drinkable as the rest. About one and a half extra bottles can be recovered in this way from a 5 gallon batch, a worthwhile recovery not only of the money involved but of the work put into the process.

Maturing period

Make plenty of wine of any one kind, say five gallons, which is almost 30 bottles, so that you and yours cannot possibly drink it all in a short time. Then occasionally the odd bottle hiding in the store cupboard will elude your eagle eye, until it has served sufficient time in the cellar to become really drinkable.

Drinking wine too early leads to a very powerful knock-down effect on the drinker, and will give your wine a reputation for potency which will be at odds with its rough taste. Save face with your friends by offering them *good* wine! Assume you will mature the wine at least one year after bottling, after you have learnt to control the ecstacy of drinking three day old kit wine.

If after a year, the first bottle of a batch taste a little rough, leave the rest for a further year. You can see now why it is good to manufacture wine in enormous quantities, as then, if frustrated by not being able to drink one particular batch, why, you can turn to some other group of bottles!

Time works wonders; kit wines as well as your fruit wines can certainly improve over four year's storage, although the colour of some reds might deteriorate.

Labelling and storage

Your corked wine bottles may have splashes on the outside which would dry in a sticky, unpleasant film. So wipe them with a clean, damp rag and put aside to dry.

Use foil caps over the bottle necks, especially if the bottles are to be stored on their sides. Such storage will keep the corks damp and tight-fitting, but can allow moulds to grow on the top of the corks in the absence of the caps. I am not sure why the foil caps do not trap moisture on the cork top and thus promote mould growth, but it is a matter of observation that caps prevent the problem. If bottles are stored upright, the caps dry out somewhat, so mould growth cannot be a problem, although the corks may tend to dry and become a little loose.

If after a year, the first bottle of a batch tastes a little rough, leave only down each vertical side. This method will make it *much* easier to wash the label off when the wine is finished.

If you sense that the risk of sediment formation in the wine on storage is quite high, then you cannot really offer the bottle to serve from at table. In this case there is no point in spending money on fancy labels which only you will see. Instead, use purely functional labels for your guidance in the cellar. The small self-adhesive ones on a backing paper are very suitable, provided they are applied only to a bone-dry surface. They stick so well indeed that the only sure way to remove them completely when washing up the bottle is to use a nylon scouring pad, or the thick type of proprietary window cleaner. A rub with surgical spirit, followed by a soapy cloth and drying, will remove any sticky left-overs.

If your storage conditions for the bottles are poor (for example, bottles stored in a garage may suffer extensive condensation on a mild Winter's day) then definitely use these self-adhesive labels, as they will not soften and fall off, neither do they support mould growth, any surface dirt being easily rubbed away so you can read it.

Under damp conditions, both ball-point and fountain pen inks fade in a few months. A sure-fire marker which is unaffected by any conditions is a thick graphite pencil of the sort used by newsagents and carpenters.

Mark on the label the type of wine it is, such as apple, redcurrant or what-have-you, only using abbreviations which you will be able to interpret months afterwards. Assume that grape is present anyway, so you do not need to mention this unless you make pure grape wine in several varieties. Mark on the label the month, and a year ahead of the time when you killed the yeast with Campden tablets, thus commencing the maturing process. Then later, when browsing through the cellar, when you see a marked date which has already passed, you will know that the wine is at least a year old and should be in a drinkable state. If you wish to boast about how old the wine is which your friends are drinking, just add one year to what is written on the label, and there you are. I find this "drink-after" method of labelling much easier to use than labelling with the date of manufacture. The further past the marked date you are, the better the wine should be. When large quantities are made, you can afford to secrete a few bottles aside from the main store, for example in a cardboard wine carton, and so reduce the temptation to drink all of one kind of wine before some of it has reached the right degree of antiquity.

If on storage your mistakes find you out, and a secondary fermentation takes place, corks will pop out of bottles stored upright, but you will still have the contents intact for corrective action, assuming you have found out soon enough and the wine is still good. If corks pop from bottles on their sides, you have lost the wine and have a horrendous mess to clear up to boot. Proper use of Campden tablets should take care of secondary fermentations; if it does occur and your wet and swollen corks hold in place, you will have a very acceptable sparkling wine as a reward for your luck.

Serving

Wine, bottled as soon as it is clear, will readily deposit a sediment on storage. In the case of pure grape wine, this is a hard, heavy, crystalline, crusty material known as ''tartar''. Its presence in your wine at public serving time shows authenticity and can be a talking point amongst guests. However, most deposits are more or less fluffy, and can easily be stirred up. Their presence in a bottle offered at table is both questionable and unappetising. So too might be a tattered or dirty label which may show evidence of unsuitable storage conditions.

The solution is to take a working stock of bottles from your store, turn them on their axis once or twice to loosen sediment on the bottle side, (which was the bottom when the bottle was laid horizontally), and stand them upright indoors in a cupboard. In a day or two, the wine is clear and can be decanted into a serving bottle, decanter or jug. It looks impressive at a dinner party if you produce a gallon bottle of your wine at table. As the serving container will be unlabelled, you can expatiate on the type of wine it is during the meal.

The operation of decanting will leave you with sediment mixed with a little cloudy, but otherwise good, wine. Keep these sediments, mixing them together in a wine bottle which is well corked. Different types of wine finding their way into this bottle will react together and the sediment will often compact down nicely. The clear wine so obtained can be used in a number of ways:

1. Use it for cooking.
2. Use it as the basis for punch, either hot or cold.
3. Add it to a larger batch of wine which is in process of being clarified ready for bottling. Do *not* add it to a fermenting ''must'' on account of the inhibitive Campden content.
4. Reserve it for your own private drinking. It will keep for several weeks despite having been opened, unlike commercial wines which will keep only for very few days once opened.

Some books suggest that red wines should be uncorked and left to stand for an hour or more before serving, "to vent off foul gases". If you have evidence of foul gases, then you have made foul wine! However, it is true to say that many red wines, and especially elderberry, benefit from reaction with air. Try storing them in a glass decanter with a poorly fitting glass stopper for about one month, so that air has a chance to react with the esters present. The result is a richer flavour. Elderberry wine can, if originally very strong, taste almost like port after this treatment.

Temperature of serving is a matter of taste. In an emergency when white wine is suddenly called for, chill in a freezer for a few minutes before serving. Avoid keeping white wine in a refrigerator indefinitely as a prelude to serving; it will be too cold for the real flavour to be appreciated. Wrapping the bottle in newspaper prior to cooling in the refrigerator is sometimes suggested in books, but seems a troublesome and poor alternative to having a quick and controlled cool. Homemade wines, full bodied as they are when made with some grape content, seem to be less sensitive to serving temperature than are commercial wines.

On cold nights, try mulling your red wine by heating it in a saucepan, or by quenching a red-hot poker in it. The resulting hot brew is comforting and incredibly potent.

A wide variety of mixed punches can be made with homemade wine, and can be used as a disguise in some cases. For example, if fruit is added, it does not matter if the wine was slightly cloudy in the first place! Elderberry wine is very good for making punch, and can be used effectively even when very new. Other red wines should undergo the standard maturing period before use in a punch.

Once opened, the wine will keep for some weeks, so there is no problem in decanting into really large bottles, as long as dust or fruit flies do not get in. I personally use a rather ornamental one (U.S.) gallon bottle which once contained Californian wine, and this is very convenient for table use, the wine lasting some weeks without ever going bad.

Dealing with problems

If you make wine my way you won't have many. If wine, old or new, starts fermenting again, and "pops" corks, then take it all out of the bottles and return to a fermentation tank. Make up a solution of Campden tablets in hot water in the usual way, and add to the wine at the rate of one tablet for each gallon. Stir in well and allow to stand for a few hours to see whether any sediment is likely to form from the small amount of yeast you have just killed. If some does come down, rack off the wine and return to the bottles so recently emptied (without an intermediate washing-up). Use new corks and finish as usual.

Some kit wines, particularly claret, can start fermenting very violently and will pour out of the airlock. Be prepared to catch it at an early stage by having a larger fermentation vessel ready or, alternatively, stand the fermentation vessel on a large tray to catch the surplus. Do not return this spillage to the ''must''.

If your wine becomes ropy or sour, I would be inclined to throw it away. Some books give details of recovery processes, but the cause is bacterial infection, which does not sound very appetising, even if you can overcome the appearance factor.

If you leave wine standing for too long over a yeast sediment, a bacterial action may occur which produces the smell of bad eggs. If you detect this problem, there are two ways of proceeding:

1. If no Campden tablets have yet been added, rack the wine, add 1 oz. of sugar to the gallon and some fresh yeast. Fermentation will start up again and the carbon dioxide gas produced will sweep the offending smell out of the wine. You can then carry on with the process as normal.

2. If Campden tablets have already been added you will not be able to get fermentation going again. So use some real chemistry. Make a solution of one tablet in a little hot water and add to the racked wine in a bucket. Can you still smell bad eggs? If so, add a second Campden dose in the same way. Allow a few minutes after each addition for the reaction to go to completion, and add the tablets successively until the smell has gone. What happens is that the bad-egg gas reacts with the choking sulphur-smelling gas from the Campden tablet to produce sulphur and water. The sulphur comes down with the dead yeast cells during the clarification process, but is totally harmless anyway.

If you have other problems, consult a more detailed book or a knowledgeable friend. Be prepared in the last resort to throw the offending wine away; after all, even good cooks have the occasional failure! It is better to make the clean break than to struggle with an inadequate wine which might put you off making more.

Problems with secondary fermentation

Very occasionally some live yeasts – resistant strains perhaps – will survive the Campden tablet treatment and transfer into the bottled wine. If they do, they can in a sufficiently sweet wine begin a second fermentation. This usually happens during the Spring following the time when you made the wine; this time will be around the Autumn if fruit was used as the basis. The yeast feeds on breakdown products from the first fermentation: whilst not much action could occur, enough gas can be generated to make the wine sparkling, which may be considered a good thing, or so much gas might be produced that corks start to blow out. So look at the neck end of your store of bottles in the spring when the garden starts to come alive, and see whether the foil caps are showing signs of being distorted because of rising corks. If such signs are there, use these bottles first if possible, and you will be rewarded with a refreshing, sparkling drink. If you consider that the action is modest, as shown by the occasional rising bubble, uncork the bottle and transfer the wine without contamination to a champagne-type bottle so that the (specially long) cork can be wired in. Ordinary wine bottles should not, not, not be expected to stand this sort of gas pressure. If you think that the secondary fermentation is altogether too much, then put all the wine back into a large vessel, add one or two Campden tablets to the gallon, depending whether the wine is white or red, rack off after settling, and rebottle in the normal way.

A way to reduce the likelihood of unwanted fermentations is to make the wine fairly dry. This means that the yeast runs completely out of food and settles out naturally when fermentation is complete. Then rack off the clearish wine from the lees before adding the Campden tablet. In this way the Campden treatment does not add any unnecessary sulphur dioxide to the wine, but that which *is* there has less yeast to work on, so is correspondingly more lethal.

Some reliable recipes

Although I set out to write this book without including recipes in it, the temptation could not be resisted to list just a few which I make repeatedly and which are found to work quite reliably. Obviously everyone has their own favourite sources of fruit, flowers or roots for making wine, but most people have access to apples, elderberries, plums and rhubarb, so I have included recipes on these starting materials. Other ones which have interesting flavours, or which offer a useful talking point at a table, involve those from your own grapes, from Jerusalem artichoke, coffee and white beam.

The assumption is made that having read the book, you will have some reasonable idea of the sequence of processes for wine making, so no great detail is given. In each case, however, the list of ingredients is what is needed to make one gallon of wine, and you merely have to multiply up according to the chosen amount of fruit you have, or wine you intend to make.

1. APPLE

Apple wine is nothing at all like cider, and only on rare occasions will it taste like apple at all. My personal experience is making with dessert apples, since these are sweeter than the cooking variety. The following recipe for dry apple wine avoids one of the problems which is encountered in some other apple-using recipes, which is to put too much apple into it. Experience shows that no more than six pounds of apples per gallon of water can be accommodated when the fruit is first crushed, otherwise a large proportion of the fruit stays out in the air and its flavour never gets extracted. It is better to be content with six pounds per gallon and to make up the flavour, as always, with white grape concentrate. The following ingredients are needed:

6 lbs good eating quality apples (no bruising or windfall damage)
½ pint white grape juice concentrate
2 lbs white sugar
2 tblspns pectolytic enzyme
½ tspn nutrient crystals
1 tspn citric acid
General purpose yeast
Water to one gallon – eventually.

Crush the apples as explained earlier in the book, using a baulk of timber and a bucket as a container. Add these to 7 pints of water containing the citric acid and the pectolytic enzyme. Cover the vessel and leave in a warm place for 48 hours, stirring at least twice daily to submerge the top layer of fruit which otherwise floats in the air. Next day, stir in the grape juice concentrate, nutrient and yeast. Ferment on the pulp until the apples soften and begin to settle out, which will take 7–10 days. Stir frequently. At the end of this time, strain the whole lot through a coarse nylon bag and squeeze it hard to extract all the liquid possible. Place the semi-dry mass into half-a-pint of water, stir around and strain again. In this way all the coarse fruit is held in the bag and what passes through is fine apple pulp and the surplus yeast. Continue fermenting under an air lock until all action ceases. Then add one Campden tablet dissolved in a little water, allow to settle, rack and bottle in the usual way.

You will find that this apple wine has a very bulky lees and this will mean that your yield is likely to be less because the sediment does not settle down and pack hard. Without having tried it, I cannot comment on the suggestion that an element of barley in this wine aids clarification and settlement, but it is certainly true that unless the pectolytic enzyme has a good opportunity to work, you will finish up with a hazy wine.

2. COFFEE

This is an interesting wine which does taste a little like coffee, but less so as it matures. If drunk at only one year old after bottling, the coffee flavour may be rather too much for some, but this matures well so that after two years or more it makes a very pleasant drink indeed, and can cause some raised eyebrows at the dinner table.

8 oz bottle of coffee essence
1 pint white grape juice concentrate
2 lbs brown sugar
1 tspn tannin solution
2 tspns citric acid
½ tspn nutrient crystals
General purpose yeast

Dissolve the sugar in two quarts of warm water and allow to cool to blood heat before adding the other ingredients and topping up to one gallon. This can be fermented in the usual way and finished at a specific gravity of 1.006 by adding two Campden tablets to kill the yeast and allow settlement. This wine comes out quite clear without any special attempts at filtration, which is a pity, because its colour is so dark that this cannot be seen by the ordinary drinker!

3. DAMSON

By damson here, I really do mean damson, and not large sloe. The sloes give a very astringent flavour to the wine which is not at all representative of good damson wine. It is best to use very juicy damsons, and so possibly it might be worth buying these rather than growing your own, unless you have a very good tree. This wine needs to be kept at least two years to reach its best flavour, but thereafter seems to be good for at least two more.

4 lbs damsons
½ pint red grape juice concentrate
2¾ lbs sugar
½ tspn tannin
½ tspn nutrient crystals
2 tspns citric acid
1 tblspn pectolytic enzyme
Yeast
Water to one gallon

Boil damsons freely in 3 quarts of water to release the stones on squeezing with gloved hands after cooling. Add the pectolytic enzyme and put in the fermenting vessel. The enzyme should be allowed at least two days to work before the other ingredients are added. Because fermentation will be very fast at first, leave plenty of head space in your vat, and because of this fast fermentation add 1½ pounds of the sugar on the first occasion and then work by the hydrometer.

Towards the end of fermentation the reaction can be very slow; it is as well not to add too much sugar at a time in case the fermentation sticks and you finish with undrinkable, very sweet liquid. After the first fermentation has died down, add the remainder of the sugar, one quarter of a pound at a time, and keep your hydrometer readings going to check that the sugar is being consumed throughout the process. After two weeks' fermentation on the pulp, strain out through a coarse nylon bag and top up with cold water and continue fermentation in the usual way. Stop the reaction with two Campden tablets before racking a few days later.

4. ELDERBERRY

This wine, which I tend to make sweet and very strong, improves considerably from the time of bottling up to at least four years old. A good tip here is to expose it to air in a decanter about three-quarters full when, after a month or so, the flavour takes on some of the qualities of port. However, the new wine is very satisfactory as the basis for making fruit punches, provided one dilutes it sufficiently with fruit juice, lemonade, etc.

You will notice that elderberry bushes come in different forms. Some of them have very wide-spread fruiting heads while others have close bunches of fruit. Some have green stems and others have red. The best variety to pick from are those with the red stems to the fruit, and with large fruits. It is quite satisfactory to mix fruit from different bushes, but the bigger berries are easier to break up in the first part of the process, in order to release the juice.

3½ lbs fresh elderberries
½ pint red grape-juice concentrate
2¾ lbs brown sugar
½ tspn nutrient crystals
2 tspns citric acid
Yeast
Water to one gallon.

Strig the fruit with a fork and add it to 3 quarts of boiling water. When this cools, break the berry skins by a washing action when using gloved hands immersed in the liquid. Add the other ingredients but only 2 lbs of the brown sugar. Allow to ferment in the usual way and add the rest of the sugar when the specific gravity has reached, say, 1.030. With care, as fermentation proceeds, more and more sugar can be added in 2 oz lots to gradually increase the alcohol content until the yeast is almost killed by it. Do this with discretion otherwise you will finish up with an unfermentable wine which is too sweet. Add two Campden tablets when fermentation is over (specific gravity 1.00 to 1.012 according to taste), and rack in the usual way.

5. ELDERFLOWER

I have no experience of making elderflower wine from the dried flowers, but the bushes available with flowers in the Spring are incredibly full of scent. If one picks the flowers on a dry, sunny day when they are totally ripe and about to fall, then no more than one pint of lightly compacted flowers is necessary for each gallon of wine. Use of any more means that the wine can be so floral that it is almost like drinking perfume, and should really need dilution with plain white wine to make it acceptable.

1 pint freshly picked elder flowers lightly compacted down
1 pint white grape juice concentrate
2 tspns citric acid
2 lbs sugar
½ tspn tanning
½ tspn nutrient crystals
General purpose yeast
Water to one gallon

Pour two quarts of boiling water on to the flowers and stir at intervals until cold and thereafter for four days. Then add the acid and sugar dissolved in a further quart of water, and when cool strain on to it the water with which the flowers have been extracted. Add the remaining ingredients, top up to almost one gallon and ferment in the usual way to specific gravity 1.006. Then add one Campden tablet, make up to one gallon and allow to settle for racking. The flavour improves after one year's storage, which should be the minimum time to be considered for this wine.

6. GRAPE

The value of commercially bought grape juice concentrates in the form of kits for wine making has been stressed in the earlier part of this book, and this is the way in which the absolute beginner should start. However, if you are lucky enough to have your own grapes, then there is no substitute for using the real fruit for the job. In general, you may find that grapes grown outside are too acid for wine making use, and may even never properly ripen. However, grapes grown under glass can be very good indeed, and in a good year the specific gravity of the juice can be as high as 1.075, although values down to 1.060 are quite common. Thus with grape wine making, very little sugar needs to be added. Grape is a marvellous wine to make because the liquid ferments very fast and cleanly, so that after ten to fourteen days you have a complete wine ready to rack and bottle without need for much sugar, and certainly no need for grape juice concentrate or any other ingredient except the starting yeast.

However, there is a point with the colour. In northern climes such as ours, even black grapes such as Hamburg never have enough colour in the skin to give more than a pale rosé coloured wine. Apparently, even the French with their more southerly vinyards have to import Algerian red grape juice to achieve the deep red colours which we associate with some of the Burgundies, etc.

10 lbs grapes taken from the stems
Sugar as necessary
Yeast.

In this recipe, we add no water to the grapes. These are broken up as explained earlier in the book, using a paint mixing paddle and power drill to give a thick liquid. You must check the specific gravity of the clear part of this liquid, in order to decide how much sugar to add so that the fermentation can begin at a specific gravity 1.080. The hydrometer does not perform properly in the thick liquid obtained by breaking down grapes, so it is best to strain some of the liquid through a wire flour sieve in order to obtain some of the real juice free of skins and gelatinous pulp. Although the grapes would ferment on their own if left, you must always observe the requirement for exclusion of air and it is far safer if general purpose yeast is added to start off the fermentation. So produce the juice by crushing, add sufficient sugar and yeast, and leave it to go. You will find that it will take at least two days before fermentation appears to have started, but thence on the fermentation will go very fast. Stir every day, leaving the skins in the liquid, which will quite suddenly become much thinner after eight to ten days and is then easier to filter. I normally ferment on the pulp for two weeks and then strain through a coarse nylon bag and continue fermentation to dryness. It is quite possible, of course, to add enough sugar to obtain a specific gravity of 1.120 or so to achieve a very high alcohol content, but here again I suggest adding sugar in small 2-oz amounts, so that if the fermentation stops before you want it to, the final wine is not too sweet and is probably still drinkable.

For safety's sake, conclude the fermentation by adding a Campden tablet prior to racking and bottling. However, if the specific gravity is about 1.006 and the fermentation is very low, you may care to experiment in racking off the almost clear liquid and bottling this with very well fitting corks. A little fermentation would then continue, giving you a sparkling wine in a year's time. However, in this case you should note that there would be a little yeast deposit in the bottom of the bottle, which you have to take care of when serving.

On storage, this wine will very often deposit crusts of tartar in the bottles, but if disturbed this settles very quickly and is, of course, a sign of authenticity of the wine to your drinking friends.

7. JERUSALEM ARTICHOKE

These root vegetables are acceptable to some people when cooked with a savoury meal, while others prefer to drink them as I do. Small mis-shapen roots can be used for wine making, while the larger and better formed ones, of course, could find their way to the dining table. In either event dig up the roots and scrub them, pulling off the hairy rootlets from them.

4 lbs artichokes
2½ lbs sugar
½ pint grape juice concentrate
1 oz powdered ginger
½ tspn tannin
½ tspn nutrient crystals
Rind and juice of 3 small lemons
Yeast

The artichokes should be broken up by passing through an ordinary kitchen mincer. When doing this wear rubber gloves, as the juice can stain your hands brown and takes a long time to wear off. Thinly pare the lemons, add the ginger powder, 2 quarts of water and the artichokes, and boil for half an hour. Then strain and dissolve in the sugar while the liquid is hot. When cool, add the grape juice concentrate, lemon juice, tannin, nutrient and yeast. Top up with cold water and ferment in the ordinary way under an air lock. After stopping with a Campden tablet at the end of fermentation, racking and bottling, you finish up with a pale amber coloured wine which is very heavy bodied, rather like an Oloroso sherry. This forms a good wine as a talking point, but is normally too full of flavour for unbridled drinking.

8. PLONK

By "plonk" one normally means cheap foreign wine which may be named "Wine of the House" in some restaurants. I use the term to indicate a mixed wine of uncertain parentage. Very little experience of wine making will show you that when racking wines you obtain quite a lot of wet sludge (lees) which in some cases, as with apple, may be very bulky. This material is not properly filterable but holds a lot of wine which, if separated, could be perfectly useful for cooking if not for drinking. Since you will have spent much time and money to get this far, there is no point in wasting anything usable from these lees. Also, when bottling you will frequently find that you have a little wine over which will not completely fill even half a bottle, and as has been said earlier in the book, it is dangerous to have too large a head space in your wine, as the flavour is adversely affected.

So, you will best be advised to consider making plonk by mixing up all your odds and scraps of liquid and lees at the end of a wine making session in order to obtain some drinkable liquid from it. It is best, for this reason, always to be fermenting at least two different kinds of wine simultaneously, so that the lees can be mixed at the end. It is an observed fact that when you mix lees from different fermentations, they tend to settle and pack much better than they will do individually, so this is what you do. You can then decant off the still somewhat cloudy mixed wine and use a close-mesh filter bag to strain the compacted yeast to obtain a little more liquid from the mixture. Repeated settlings and decanting in this way will give you quite a passable drink to which you can add any residual good wine which you have been unable to squeeze into your existing bottling programme. However, do not be too enthusiastic and be tempted to mix more than two different kinds of wine in order to make a bottle of plonk. Once too many scraps are included, then the flavour does suffer. You should also not reduce your standards of manufacture and cleanliness, and should not be tempted to rebottle new wine which has been standing out in the air for two or three days, because of possible problems with vinegar flies and oxidation. You will find, however, that the plonk you make has one advantage, which is that after a year's storage it generally turns up star bright without any special filtration or other treatment. As always, keep it at least a year and label it "plonk" so as not to confuse the innocent drinker.

9. PLUM

Plums are famous for their pectin. This is a big hazard to the wine maker, since even with a lot of effort using pectolytic enzyme you can still find a slight haze in the wine. A friend gave me a good tip once, which was that they serve their plum wine in a non-transparent (such as metal) goblet, so that the drinker cannot see the product!

5 lbs fresh plums
½ pint red grape juice concentrate
2¼ lbs sugar
½ tspn tannin
1 tspn citric acid
½ tspn nutrient crystals
3 tblspns pectolytic enzyme
General purpose yeast
2 Campden tablets
Water to one gallon.

Wash the plums and pour on two quarts of boiling water. When cool, mash the mixture with your hands and remove the stones. Stir in the citric acid, tannin and pectolytic enzyme and leave in a warm place for three days, stirring occasionally. Next day, stir in the grape juice concentrate, sugar, nutrient and yeast. Ferment on the pulp for seven days then strain through a coarse-mesh nylon bag. Make up to volume, fit the airlock and ferment as usual to dry or sweet as required. This wine is best if kept for two years, during which time it also has some chance to settle out if at all hazy when bottled. An alternative way of dealing with the haze is to blend it with another wine such as apple, which gives the same problem, and here lies a fruitful field for experimentation.

10. RHUBARB

See the text in earlier sections regarding the preparation of the fruit in order to extract the juice from it. You really do need a freezer for this activity, but should be able to obtain the use of one from a friend or neighbour if you do not possess your own. If one boils the fruit as recommended in many other recipes, one can tend to get a very hazy wine which is difficult to clear by any known means other than blending. The rhubarb is easily obtained from your own garden or from a pick-it-yourself farm, but should be picked during late May on a dry day. Trim off the white base and also the leaf, and go for the thick stalks as these are easier to deal with.

5 lbs rhubarb
½ pint white grape juice concentrate
2¼ lbs sugar
½ tspn nutrient crystals
2 tblspns pectolytic enzyme
General purpose yeast
1 Campden tablet
Thinly pared rind of a large lemon

Extract the juice by freezing the sticks, thawing in a bucket and rolling out the limp stems with a rolling pin in a water-tight tray. Make up the liquid to seven pints with cold water, if possible using the new water to wash additional juice from the exhausted stems. Add the thinly pared rind of lemon and the pectolytic enzyme, leaving covered for 48 hours. Then stir in the grape juice, sugar, nutrient and yeast, and ferment to dryness.

11. TEA

Some recipes tell you to keep the dregs from the teapot and combine these until you have a gallon, thus enough to make wine. While I have done this myself, it is not very appetising in the collecting stage and can take quite a long time to collect a gallon, particularly if you are an avid coffee drinker, so it is best to use ten tea bags for each gallon and freshly brew them in a saucepan by simmering.

10 tea bags
½ pint white grape juice concentrate
2 lbs sugar
½ tspn nutrient crystals
2 tsps citric acid
General purpose yeast
Water to one gallon.

Extract the tea bags with 3 quarts of boiling water and after two minutes remove them and stir in the sugar and acid. When cool add the grape juice, nutrient and yeast, top up with water and ferment as usual. This provides a refreshing drink with a curious tea colour unlike most other wines.

12. WHITE BEAM

You may not be familiar with white beam. It is a tree common on chalk in southern England but localised in distribution all over, and is a member of the rose family with the Latin name Sorbus Aria. It forms a very ornamental tree with brilliant pink blossom like the flowering cherry in the spring, and big dark red fruit like rose-hips in the autumn. The wine is very clear and is an unusual shade of bright light red, which is a good talking point for the drinker.

4½ lbs white beam hips
½ pint white grape juice concentrate
2½ lbs sugar
½ tspn tannin
2 tbspns pectolytic enzyme
2 tspns citric acid
General purpose yeast
½ tspn nutrient crystals
1 Campden tablet
Water

Wash and crush the hips and pour on 2 quarts of boiling water. When cool add the tannin and pectolytic enzyme, leaving covered for two days. Then stir in the grape juice concentrate, nutrient and yeast Ferment on the pulp for a week and then strain thoroughly through a wire flour sieve. Stir in the sugar, top up with water and continue fermentation to specific gravity something below 1.012. Rack after adding one Campden tablet and bottle in the usual way. Again you need at least one year's storage before drinking. If you cannot get white beam, try this recipe with rose hips.

You will notice in all the above recipes that unless grape is the main fruit ingredient, more or less grape juice concentrate is used. Where elderflowers, for example, are used as the flavouring they have no sugar in themselves, so essentially one has to make up a wine from grape juice concentrate and use the flowers only for flavouring. In other cases, as with damson, the fruit itself is adequate for making a certain amount of body and flavour in the wine, so that the amount of concentrate to be added is less. Reiterating what was said earlier in the book, one should always have some grape content in a wine to give it the right body and something like the right kind of flavour.

It is recommended that for white wines one should have sufficient sugar added throughout the course of the fermentation to have yielded an initial specific gravity of 1.080 if all the sugar were added at once. Nearly all the sugar, or maybe quite all of it, is fermented out during the process, but by using Campden tablets when the specific gravity has reached the right figure (1.012 for sweet wines, 1.006 for medium wines and 1.000 or less for dry wines) you can finish up with wine of the flavour you like. Generally, red wines are stronger than white and I would recommend using enough sugar to give you, effectively, a starting specific gravity of 1.110, but to avoid over-burdening the yeast it might be desirable to add this sugar in two or more quantities to make up the full amount.

Information sources and reading list

Your best source of practical tips is this book. You must believe that, to have bought it. For the theory of wine making and specifically for more recipes, there are many books on the market, and a few of them are listed at the end of this section. Some books identify recipes by the type of fruit which is to be used, for example medlar or blackberry. Others tell you how, by using the correct fruit and the right method, to simulate a well-known commercial type of wine. Thus rhubarb can be used as the basis for simulated hocks. Don't fool yourself. You may be able to make superb wines, the like of which cannot be obtained in the market place, but you will never be able to make a Bordeaux like the French professionals do. So do not go in for vain competition, but do the things which you can do best.

Remember to use the special gravity table: these measurements are *vital*; we have all tasted country-style homemade wines which were fermented by guesswork. The liquid may have been flavoured water, or at the other extreme have been as strong as aviation spirit; either case does not leave the drinker with the confident impression that the wine producer knew what he was doing.

The following books represent a small cross section of those currently on the market: mention here does not imply specific recommendation.

1. "Growing vines" by Nick Poulter. Standard Press AW Publications Ltd., Andover, Hants.
2. "Progressive Winemaking" by B. Acton & P. Duncan, AW Publications Ltd, Andover, Hants.
3. "First steps in wine making" by C. J. J. Berry. AW Publications Ltd., Andover, Hants.
4. "Beginners book of home wine-making" by Ben Turner. Wolfe Publishing Ltd, Conway Street, London.
5. "Boots book of home wine and beer making" by Ben Turner. Wolfe Publishing Ltd, Conway Street, London.
6. "Wine making at home" by Francis Pinnegar. Hamlyn Publishing Group, Feltham, Middlesex.

INDEX